YouTube Secrets Revealed: Master the Algorithm, Boost Your Views, and Monetize Like a Pro

Micheal .E. Hunt

All right reserved. No part of this book publication may be reproduced, distributed or transmitted in any form or by any means, including photocopying, recording or other electronic or mechanical methods, without prior written permission of the publisher, except in the case of brief quotations embodied in critical reviews and certain other non commercial uses permitted by copyright laws

Copyright © 2024

INTRODUCTION

YouTube provides a fantastic platform for creativity, influence, and enterprise in the modern digital age. This tutorial will walk you through all of the crucial actions and approaches required to launch and expand a profitable YouTube channel.

It's thrilling and difficult to become a successful YouTuber in a time when digital media rules and the pull of internet celebrity is stronger than ever. The path to success on YouTube requires a combination of strategy, creativity, and perseverance, regardless of whether your motivation stems from the desire to share your passion, establish a personal brand, or generate income.

Greetings and welcome to "YouTube Secrets Revealed: Master the Algorithm, Boost Your Views, and Monetize

Like a Pro". This book is meant to serve as your all-inclusive guide through the colorful and exciting world of YouTube. This book provides insights and useful suggestions to help you manage the complexities of the platform, regardless of your level of expertise in creating videos or whether you're a rookie looking to hone your craft.

YouTube is a potent instrument for influence, community development, and narrative in addition to being a place where videos may be uploaded. The competition is tough, with over 2 billion monthly log-in users and a wide range of content categories. But you can carve out your niche, attract a committed audience, and accomplish your goals with the appropriate tactics, resources, and mindset.

This book will help you learn about:
-Understanding the Platform
- Learn how to take advantage of YouTube's monetization policies and algorithms by developing a thorough understanding of the ecosystem.

- Planning Your Channel, Accomplish goals that are in line with your vision, develop a content plan, and establish your brand.

 - Content Creation: Learn the fundamentals of video production, from tools and methods to developing gripping storylines that enthrall viewers.

- Building Your Audience: Learn the subtleties of YouTube SEO, successful marketing techniques, and how to interact with your audience to create a devoted following.

- Monetisation and Growth: Investigate different revenue streams, methods for channel scalability, and approaches to maintain motivation and prevent burnout.

- Legal and Ethical Considerations: Make sure you uphold integrity and compliance by navigating the complexity of copyright, privacy, and ethical content creation.

Every chapter has been carefully written to give you useful advice, doable suggestions, and real-world examples. By the time you finish reading this guide, you'll know exactly what it takes to be successful on

YouTube and have all the resources you need to realize your dreams. Set out on this adventure with an open mind and a readiness to change and grow. Opportunities and obstacles abound on the road to YouTube success, but with the correct information and commitment, you can leave your imprint and create a successful channel.

TABLE OF CONTENT

INTRODUCTION

CHAPTER 1: THE YOUTUBE ECOSYSTEM

    Knowing YouTube's Requirements and Policies for Monetisation

    Identifying your Niche

    Analyzing Market Demand and Competition

CHAPTER 2: PLANNING YOUR CHANNEL

    Establishing Objectives for Your YouTube Channel

CHAPTER 3 : CONTENT CREATION

    Crafting Compelling Videos: The Art of Engaging Storytelling

CHAPTER 4: BUILDING YOUR AUDIENCE

    Marketing Your Channel

    Creating a Connection and Loyalty with Your Audience

CHAPTER 5: MONETIZING YOUR CHANNEL: DIVERSE STRATEGIES FOR REVENUE GENERATION

    Maintaining Motivation and Preventing Burnout:

CHAPTER 6: LEGAL AND ETHICAL CONSIDERATION

- What is copyright ?
- Handling Privacy and Security
- Ethical Content Creation

CHAPTER 1: THE YOUTUBE ECOSYSTEM

Think of YouTube as a thriving online city where each video is a colorful shop in an expansive marketplace. YouTube's algorithms act as the intelligent traffic cops and powerful curators of the city in an ever-changing landscape, directing users to the material they are most likely to find entertaining and engaging. To make sure your films stand out and get the attention they deserve, rather than merely blending into the pack, it's imperative to understand these algorithms.

A).The YouTube Recommendation Engine: Nickname "The Guardians of Visibility".The recommendation engine of YouTube is the fundamental component of its content discovery system. Imagine this as a complex network of links that is always updating itself in response to user activity. This engine kicks in once a viewer completes a video, offering a customized list of recommendations based on their viewing interests and behaviors. Your content needs to align with the viewer's interests and interaction style to show up in these recommendations. This implies that the descriptions, thumbnails, and titles of your videos must correctly and compellingly convey the content. The algorithm is more likely to recommend a video if it has a lot of likes, comments, and shares.

B).The Digital Librarian of YouTube(The Search Algorithm):Think of the YouTube search algorithm as the platform's digital library, methodically cataloging the extensive collection of videos. This algorithm examines the metadata, including titles, tags, and descriptions, when a user types in a search query and determines how closely your movie matches the query terms. Your content needs to be optimized for relevant keywords and phrases if you want it to stand out in search results. Use precise keywords, write interesting and educational descriptions, and make sure the title of your movie accurately conveys what it is about. Your metadata has a greater chance of showing up in search results if it is more precise and relevant.

(C) The Metric of Engagement(YouTube's Quality Control):The algorithm uses engagement to determine how appealing and high-quality your video is. Consider it as the YouTube quality control staff, assessing how users engage with your material. Prominent metrics like watch duration, likes, comments, and shares indicate favorably to the algorithm. Provide engaging material that draws viewers in and promotes participation from the outset. Make use of captivating openings, ask probing questions, and include calls to action. YouTube receives a stronger signal that your film is worthy of promotion the longer visitors stay on the page and the more they interact.

(D) The Watch History and Customisation(The Personalised Touch of the Algorithm): Additionally, recommendations are tailored by YouTube's algorithm according to each user's viewing history. Think of it like a tailor creating a personalized viewing experience for each person. Because of this personalization, even if your video is a great fit for a larger audience, you still need to interact with your current subscribers and viewers to increase the likelihood that similar new users will see it and promote it to them. Promote subscriptions and cultivate a devoted audience. Regular visitors to your channel tell YouTube's algorithm that your material is worthwhile and pertinent.

(E) The Factor of Freshness(Maintaining Up-to-Date in a Quickly Changing World): In the always-changing world of YouTube, newness counts. Content that draws from current events or popular trends is given a boost by the algorithm, which keeps track of hot themes and recent uploads. Maintaining timely and relevant material might help you become more visible. Maintaining relevance and drawing in viewers requires striking a balance between timeless content and current issues. You can guarantee that the proper audience sees and actively promotes your videos by being aware of and utilizing

YouTube's algorithms. Accept the intricacy of these digital systems and make use of them to direct your content strategy and raise your profile in the busy metropolis of YouTube.

Knowing YouTube's Requirements and Policies for Monetisation

Understanding the rules of a challenging game is similar to navigating the YouTube monetization landscape. Knowing these guidelines as a content creator guarantees that your work complies with YouTube's standards and also opens up the possibility of earning money. This is a thorough analysis of YouTube's monetization guidelines and requirements to assist you in profitably converting your passion. The YouTube Partner Program (YPP) is your entry point to income. You must be a member of the YouTube Partner Program (YPP) to directly monetize your videos through advertisements. The first step to getting access to extra monetization features and making money from advertisements is to sign up for YPP.

Your channel needs to fulfill certain requirements to apply for YPP. These include having 4,000 watch hours over the previous 12 months, 1,000 subscribers, and an AdSense account that is connected.

Additionally, you have to abide by all of YouTube's rules and regulations. Using the YouTube Studio dashboard, apply after your channel satisfies the requirements for eligibility. YouTube will examine your channel to make sure that it complies with content policies, copyright laws, and community guidelines. Both automatic systems and human review are used in this procedure.

If approved, you'll be able to use monetization tools including channel memberships, Super Chats, and ad income. However, YouTube regularly monitors your channel to verify continuing compliance with its standards.

Once accepted into YPP, your principal revenue source will be ad revenue. This is simply the Core of Monetization. YouTube utilizes a combination of automated technology and human assessment to position adverts on your videos.

YouTube offers different ad forms, including display advertisements, overlay ads, skippable video ads, and non-skippable video commercials. The amount you make can vary based on the ad format, viewer geography, and ad demand. -

YouTube runs on a revenue-sharing arrangement. Typically, producers earn 55% of the ad money produced from their videos, while YouTube retains 45%. The actual amount you make can differ depending on various variables, including audience demographics and ad interaction. -

To maximize ad revenue, your material must be judged advertiser-friendly. This involves avoiding contentious or sensitive issues that can lead to limited or no ads.

YouTube has a set of criteria on what makes ad-friendly videos, which includes avoiding excessive language, violence, and unsuitable content.

Super Chat and Channel Memberships are yet again another source of income on the YouTube platform. YouTube provides extra monetization options in addition to standard ad revenue to help you diversify your income. With this function, viewers can subscribe to your channel every month and become paying members. Emojis, unique badges, and access to members-only content are all provided to members. Your channel needs to have over 30,000 subscribers and be at least 18 years old to allow memberships.

Viewers can buy Super Chats and Super Stickers to emphasize their messages or express support during live streaming. Channels with more than 1,000 subscribers can use this function, which allows viewers to directly donate money during in-person encounters.

After this, For approved channels, YouTube now provides a merchandising shelf where you can sell branded goods straight from your channel. Your channel must have more than 10,000 subscribers to use this function. With the help of the merchandise shelf's integration with other merchandise partners, you may display and market goods like mugs and t-shirts.

A membership program called YouTube Premium provides exclusive content, ad-free viewing, and other features. A portion of the money made by YouTube Premium subscribers who view your material is paid to you as the producer. The amount of revenue is allocated according to how long Premium members watch your content.

To keep your work monetized, you must make sure it complies with copyright regulations. The Content ID system on YouTube tracks copyright claims and checks videos for content protected by copyright. This is how monetization is impacted, The owner of the copyright may file a claim against your movie if it includes copyrighted content. As a result, the rights holder can receive the monetization revenue instead of you. Steer clear of utilizing other people's music, videos, or other content without their consent.

Under certain circumstances, you may use copyrighted content by fair use clauses. Fair use is a complicated legal topic, though, and disagreements can occur. You can challenge an allegation using YouTube's procedure if you think it's false, but be ready to defend your usage of the content.

It is imperative that you adhere to YouTube's community guidelines and policies to preserve the monetization status of your channel. The monetization functions may be suspended or demonetized as a result of violations. Crucial aspects to pay attention to mostly is Complying with YouTube's policies for misinformation, hate speech, harassment, and other forbidden material. To guarantee compliance, examine and keep current on YouTube's policies regularly.

Ensuring the safety and privacy of viewers is crucial. Refrain from divulging personal information, carrying out destructive activities, and going against privacy norms.

Optimising your monetization plan requires close observation of your earnings and channel success. Through the YouTube Studio, the platform offers comprehensive analytics that includes information on viewer demographics, revenue, and engagement data. Make the most of your earning potential by modifying your content strategy based on this data.Creating a profitable and long-lasting channel requires an understanding of YouTube's policies and standards around monetization. By fulfilling the requirements, maximizing advertising revenue, investigating different sources of income, and making sure all rules are followed, you may successfully negotiate the monetization terrain and convert your artistic endeavors into a profitable venture.

Identifying your Niche

Selecting a Specialisation That Complies with Your Interest and Experience. Choosing a specialty for your YouTube channel is similar to figuring out where you fit in a busy creative environment. Finding the sweet spot where your knowledge and enthusiasm meet to create content that speaks to both you and your audience deeply is the key. This guide will show you how to create a channel that is both interesting and gratifying by identifying the ideal location for your passion and experience.

Before choosing a specialty, consider what interests you. The motivation for consistently producing new material is your enthusiasm. To find it out. Jot down a list of the subjects that you find inspiring, whether they relate to your interests, hobbies, or career. Consider engaging in exciting hobbies, having enjoyable conversations, or researching topics regularly.

Consider if you can imagine yourself talking about this subject for many years to come. To avoid burnout and guarantee that you stay involved with your material over time, a niche should pique your continued curiosity and excitement.

Think about how the subject relates to your long-term objectives and personal values. Producing material that aligns with your principles not only sustains your motivation but also draws in visitors who share your views.

Also you should learn how to Make Use of Your Experience. Expertise gives your writing authority and credibility.

When Finding your specialty you should always consider the following; your upbringing, education, and life experiences. What are you especially good at? What expertise do you possess that would be useful to others? These could be life experiences, scholarly knowledge, or professional skills. Think about how your special viewpoint or background contributes. Do you have any unique perspectives or methods for your field that others might not? This distinctiveness can help your content stand out from the crowd.

Make use of your practical knowledge in your area. Applying your knowledge in the real world frequently yields more in-depth information than merely theoretical comprehension.

Finding the point where passion and skill converge requires a careful blending of the two. Compare and contrast your areas of expertise with your list of passions. Where your talents and interests meet, look for areas of commonality. For instance, combining your love of exercise and expertise in sports science can help you carve out an interesting and authoritative niche.

Learn how to Play around with concepts for content that connect your areas of expertise and interest. To determine how successfully you can maintain interest and engagement, make a few videos or blog entries. Take note of comments and adjust your focus according to what you and your audience find most compelling. Find out what information your possible audience is looking for. Utilise resources such as Google Trends, YouTube's search recommendations, and social media analytics to ascertain prevailing subjects in your selected field. This guarantees that there is a market for your niche in addition to it being in line with your hobbies.

Selecting a niche also entails evaluating its market potential. Look at current channels and content producers in the niche you've selected. Determine their areas of strength and potential areas for improvement or distinctiveness. A niche that allows for novel viewpoints or unusual views may hold greater potential. Consider the profitability of your selected niche. More extensive alternatives for monetization through affiliate marketing, sponsorships, and adverts are available in certain niches. Tech companies seeking influencer connections, for instance, may be drawn to technology evaluations, and niche hobbies may have specific goods to endorse.

Make sure there is space for expansion and variety within the niche. A profitable niche should support a variety of themes and content kinds, giving you the chance to gradually expand your channel's offers.

Finally, make sure the niche you've selected appeals to your target audience and permits authenticity. Remain True to Who You Are. Your content should demonstrate your enthusiasm and level of experience. Authenticity creates a real connection with your audience and helps to establish trust. If a niche doesn't mesh with your actual interests, don't choose it just because it seems profitable or in line with current trends.

Always make sure to interact with your Audience. By interacting with viewers, you can create a community around your topic. Seek their advice, answer their criticism, and make changes in response to their suggestions. Refine your specialization and increase the appeal of your channel with a responsive and interactive approach. Selecting a specialization that fits your expertise and enthusiasm is a very personal and strategic choice. It takes self-reflection to discover your motivations, a frank evaluation of your abilities, and careful consideration of market possibilities.

You may build a YouTube channel that fulfills you and engages your audience at the same time by figuring out where these components come together. This will set you up for long-term success and enjoyment.

Analyzing Market Demand and Competition

Establishing a YouTube channel requires knowing the competitors and market needs to carve out a niche that draws and keeps visitors. By examining these components, you may better recognize opportunities, foresee difficulties, and formulate strategies. To position your channel for success, follow these steps for doing in-depth and perceptive research on market demand and competition.

Firstly you need to Evaluate Consumer Demand. Measuring the amount of interest and demand for content in your selected niche is a necessary step in understanding market demand. This is how you go about it.To find popular search terms and subjects in your niche, use resources like Google Trends and YouTube's search recommendations. Examine the variations in search interest over time to ascertain whether demand is increasing, staying the same, or decreasing. Instead of focussing on ephemeral trends, look for patterns that point to sustained interest.

Websites like Reddit, Instagram, and Twitter can provide information on hot subjects and conversations. Keep an eye on hashtags, forums, and groups associated with your area of expertise to learn about the queries people are posing and the information they like. Ask questions or do interviews with prospective viewers to get their opinions straight. Enquire about their hobbies, difficulties, and favorite kinds of content via social media or internet resources. This direct feedback can highlight market gaps and confirm that there is a need for your content concepts.

Examine other videos in your niche to determine what has a strong following. Analyse popular videos' view counts, interaction data, and viewer comments. This might assist you in determining popular subjects and useful content types.

Secondly you need to gain solid grasp of Comprehending Competition. Examining competitors means assessing channels that are already in place and content producers in your market. To begin, enumerate well-known channels and content producers within your industry. Examine both well-known, established artists and up-and-coming, smaller ones. This provides you with a thorough understanding of the competitive environment.

Look at the content tactics of your rivals. Take note of their posting schedules, formats, and subjects for videos. Examine the way they interact with their audience and showcase their brand. Gaining insight into their methodology facilitates the identification of effective strategies and domains in which you may set yourself apart. Check out how rivals communicate with their viewers. Examine the quantity and caliber of shares, likes, comments, and other indicators of interaction. High levels of involvement can reveal what appeals to viewers and point out areas where you might need to innovate or adjust.

Look for any holes or neglected areas in the material of your rivals. If competitors, for instance, concentrate a lot of effort on one area of a niche while ignoring another, you may be able to fill that gap. You might differentiate yourself by offering original viewpoints or examining neglected subjects.

Keep tabs on the development patterns of significant rivals. Examine subscription numbers, growth rates, and content strategy modifications. Quick expansion or changes in emphasis may point to new trends or effective tactics that are worthwhile to take into account.

Thirdly, you need to Learn how to Make Use of Insights in Strategy. Once you have a firm grasp on the competition and market demand, use the following information to inform your channel strategy. Using the results of your analysis, create a special value proposition. Look for methods to differentiate yourself from rivals, whether it's by using a unique format, a particular focus, or your style. By being different, you can draw in visitors who are looking for something new and different. Make sure your content strategy takes audience interests and recognized demand trends into account. Provide original material that incorporates your viewpoint and tackles hot subjects or frequently asked issues in your niche. This guarantees the continued relevance and interest of your material. -

Base your video tags, descriptions, and titles on highly sought-after search terms by conducting keyword research. Good SEO techniques raise the visibility and searchability of your material, which raises the possibility that it will draw in more visitors. Remain adaptable and ready to modify your plan in response to developing market trends and rivalry. To improve your strategy and stay competitive, examine audience comments and performance indicators regularly.

Fourthly you must be Observant and always make room for improvement Improvement Analysis of consumer demand and rivalry in the market is still underway. Keep an eye on market developments, audience opinions, and rivalry. You may keep informed about evolving opportunities and shifting dynamics by conducting regular evaluations. Make incremental changes to your content and approach based on audience input and performance analytics insights.

To stay relevant and engaging, adjust to changing trends and viewer preferences. You can set up your YouTube channel for success by carefully examining the competition and market demand. Gaining a competitive edge by knowing your audience's preferences and how to set yourself apart from the competition will give your content a strategic edge and help it stand out in a crowded market.

CHAPTER 2:PLANNING YOUR CHANNEL

In Creating a distinct personality on YouTube you need to First define your brand. It takes more than just a name and logo to create a persona that connects with your target market and makes you stand out from the competition.You'll need to Develop an Eye-Catching Channel Name and Logo.Potential viewers will form an initial opinion of you based on your channel name. It should capture the spirit of your writing, be memorable, and be simple to spell. Begin by coming up with name ideas that capture your specialty and unique style. Think about naming your material after your unique selling proposition or theme. For example, if your channel is about eco-friendly living, a name like "GreenSteps" could succinctly communicate your dedication to sustainability.

Making a logo is the next thing you should do after deciding on a name. Your channel's theme and name should flow naturally into this visual element. In addition to being polished, a well-designed logo promotes brand identification. If your channel is about tech reviews, for instance, a sleek, contemporary logo with tech-related elements can convey your focus clearly and quickly. To make sure your logo works well on a variety of platforms, use basic, instantly recognizable colors and designs.

Learn how to Create a Visual Style and Brand Voice That Are Consistent. The foundation of how people perceive your channel is built on your brand voice and visual style. The personality and tone that emerges in your interactions and videos is your brand voice. Whether your brand voice is official and instructive or informal and funny, maintaining consistency in it can help you establish a solid rapport with your audience. For example, if your channel features motivating content, a happy, upbeat tone will fit with your goal and draw in viewers who share your interests.

Your visual style, which includes thumbnails and video aesthetics alike, reflects your brand language. By choosing a color scheme and visual components that complement your content, you may create a unified look. This could entail giving your films a unified backdrop, using particular filters or effects, and creating visually appealing thumbnails with a consistent aesthetic. A strong visual identity contributes to the professional image-building of your content by making it readily recognizable.

Establishing and preserving brand recognition requires consistency. This entails using the visual and aural components of your brand consistently throughout your channel. Make sure that every touchpoint, including your social media accounts and video intros and outros, accurately conveys your brand identity. Utilizing your logo, color scheme, and tone consistently will strengthen your brand and increase viewers' recall. To keep things consistent, think about developing a brand guide. Your channel name, logo usage, color scheme, font selections, and tone of voice should all be covered in this guide. It acts as a guide for coming up with fresh material and preserving the integrity of your brand over time. You can establish a distinctive online presence on YouTube that draws in and keeps people by thoroughly defining your brand. Building a powerful and memorable brand that sticks out in the congested YouTube scene requires an engaging channel name and logo, a consistent brand voice, and a unified visual design.

The second step is to develop a content strategy. A solid content plan is the foundation for the success of your YouTube channel. It entails creating, organizing, and distributing material that appeals to your audience and supports your objectives.

This is a thorough how-to for creating a content plan that can increase growth and engagement:

1. Choosing Your Content Objectives Clearly:
defining your content goals is essential before you start making videos. These goals will direct your actions and assist in gauging your progress. Objectives could be raising engagement levels, growing the number of

subscribers, or directing visitors to a relevant product or website. Setting quantifiable, explicit goals guarantees that each piece of content fulfills a function and advances your overarching vision.

2. Recognising Your Audience:
A comprehensive comprehension of your intended audience is essential for developing a pertinent content strategy. Investigate watching patterns, interests, and demographic information first. To learn more about who is viewing your videos and what they are interested in, use YouTube Analytics together with other tools. You can better adapt your content to the tastes and requirements of your visitors by developing thorough audience personas, which are profiles that reflect various user demographics.

3. Changing Up the Content Types
Having a wide variety of content kinds makes your channel interesting and lively. Various formats can assist you in reaching a wider audience and accommodate a range of viewing preferences. Think about

adding,Educational films Like:Explainer, tutorial, and howfilms add value and demonstrate your subject-matter experience or if. It's an Entertainment Content,you can do Reaction videos, vlogs, and challenges that can draw viewers in and give your channel a more informal, human touch. If you want to base your content on Reviews and Opinions, then you should focus on Product reviews, commentary, and opinion articles provide valuable information that may impact decisions about what to buy or initiate conversations. Also Live Streams are also important content areas that most people underrate. Direct audience involvement and community building are made possible by real-time interaction through live streams. Maintaining viewer attention and promoting various forms of interaction with your material are two benefits of balancing these formats.

4. Creating a Calendar for Content

An effective tool for planning your video production schedule and guaranteeing regular uploads is a content calendar. Create a monthly or quarterly plan.To create a consistent posting schedule, assign precise dates to each video release. Based on your audience's interests and your research, assign subjects for each date. This preparation guarantees a wide variety of themes and prevents the need for last-minute content production. Include relevant content that coincides with holidays, the news, or popular subjects. This strategy can increase engagement by leveraging the interest already held by viewers. A well-kept calendar offers an organized method for creating material and aids in workload management.

5. Keeping Trending and Evergreen Content
 In Balance Trending and evergreen material are combined in a winning strategy. Long after it is released, evergreen content still has value and draws viewers in. Comprehensive guides or basic tutorials are two examples. Conversely, trending content capitalizes on hot subjects or current events to generate traffic spikes and short-term interest. Maintaining equilibrium between these kinds guarantees that your channel stays current and draws in both new and returning viewers.

6. Search Engine Optimisation and Content For your content to become more visible and draw in more readers, search engine optimisation is essential. Put into practice efficient SEO strategies by Creating Captivating Titles, Craft intriguing and evocative titles that don't use any deceptive keywords, Writing Detailed Descriptions Include keywords and links to relevant resources in your video description to provide viewers with a comprehensive synopsis of the topic, Use Tags Strategically Add pertinent tags to enhance searchability by helping YouTube comprehend the context and content of your video and lastly Create Captivating Thumbnails Personalised thumbnails with legible text and images have a big influence on click-through rates. Optimizing your content effectively guarantees that it is seen by the appropriate people and ranks highly in search results.

7. Tracking Results and Making Adjustments Use measurement tools like YouTube Analytics to keep an eye on the performance of your material regularly. Monitor important performance metrics like engagement rates, audience retention, and watch duration. Determine what subjects and content kinds are most successful and what still needs to be improved. Be ready to modify your plan in response to performance information. If some videos receive more views or are more engaging, think about creating similar content. On the other hand, if particular formats or subjects perform poorly, evaluate and improve your strategy.

8. Taking Part in Your Community

A strong content strategy includes active community interaction in addition to development. Build a devoted following of viewers by participating in conversations, replying to comments, and soliciting feedback. Encourage a sense of connection and involvement among your audience by interacting with them on social media, holding Q&A sessions, and conducting polls.

9. Working Together with Other Creators Working together with other YouTubers can help you reach a wider audience and bring in new viewers to your channel. Collaborating with content producers in related or complementary fields yields reciprocal advantages and enhances the diversity of your offerings. Arrange joint initiatives that complement the subjects and viewership of both networks.

10. Constantly Changing

Since the digital world is always changing, your content strategy should also be flexible. Keep yourself updated about the newest techniques, tools, and trends in the YouTube ecosystem. Try a variety of content forms, strategies, and technological advancements to keep your channel interesting and lively. By creating and executing your content strategy methodically, you lay out a plan for long-term expansion and audience involvement. This methodical technique guarantees that your endeavors are in line with your overarching objectives and vision, while also improving the caliber and pertinence of your material.

Establishing Objectives for Your YouTube Channel

An essential first step in creating a successful YouTube channel is goal-setting. Well-defined, achievable objectives offer guidance, track advancement, and stimulate expansion. They assist in turning your channel from an idea into a profitable business. This comprehensive book will help you set and accomplish meaningful goals.

Establishing what you want to accomplish with your YouTube channel is the first step in creating goals. These goals ought to be clear, quantifiable, and consistent with your overarching vision. Think about segmenting your objectives into areas like engagement, content quality, and audience growth. You may decide to raise your average view count by 20%, obtain 10,000 subscribers in less than a year, or produce videos twice a week as your goal.

A popular paradigm for successful goal-setting is SMART objectives. Every objective ought to be Specific, Make sure your goals are specified. Give specific goals, such as "increase subscriber count to 5,000 within six months," as opposed to a general one like "grow my channel." Measurably, To monitor your progress, quantify your objectives. Make use of metrics like engagement rates, watch times, and views. In doing this you need to also make sure that your objectives are reasonable in light of your available resources and situation. Overly ambitious targets can cause dissatisfaction, but reasonable goals promote steady advancement. Match your objectives to your channel's niche and overarching vision. Every goal ought to support your long-term achievement. Establish a timeframe for accomplishing your objectives. A timeline helps organize chores and gives them a sense of urgency. "Gain 1,000 subscribers by the end of the next quarter," for example.

Establishing Both Short- and Long-Term Objectives is another key factor to look at. Setting both short- and long-term objectives offers a balanced strategy for development. Short-term objectives center on achievable benchmarks, including raising the frequency of weekly uploads or enhancing the caliber of video creation. Conversely, long-term objectives cover more expansive aspirations such as establishing a lucrative item line or being a well-known influencer in your industry. Setting short-term objectives helps you move closer to realizing your long-term vision. A 10% increase in monthly views on your channel, for instance, may help you achieve your main objective of 50,000 members in a year.

Setting Priorities and Ordering Objectives has proven to also be an helpful factor in establishing objectives. Prioritisation aids in the efficient management of your attention and resources because not all goals are created equal. Determine which objectives are most important for the expansion of your channel, then devote time and energy to achieving them. For example, you could give more importance to producing interactive content and raising your comment response rate if your main goal is to increase viewer engagement. Setting goals in a logical sequence in which achieving one facilitates or supports achieving another is known as sequencing. Creating a comprehensive content calendar, for instance, could make it easier to achieve your desired upload frequency, which in turn boosts subscriber counts.

Next we look at Formulating Action Plans, actionable Plans are necessary to turn objectives into reality. Divide each objective into more achievable subtasks or benchmarks. If your objective is to increase the quality of your videos, for example, your action plan may involve making an investment in better gear, taking advanced editing courses, and setting up a more formal filming location. To keep things moving forward and guarantee timely completion, give each task a deadline. To remain on course and adjust to any changes in the channel's environment, review and modify your action plans regularly

Monitoring your progress is crucial to assessing how well your plans and objectives are working. Track metrics like watch time, interaction rates, and subscriber growth using YouTube Analytics. To find out if you're on track or if changes are needed, compare your performance to your predetermined goals. Review your successes and failures regularly to learn what works and what doesn't. You may improve your tactics and make more sensible, objective-setting decisions in the future by engaging in this reflective activity.

Sometimes you should Also learn to Modify and Review of Objectives. Because YouTube is a dynamic platform, objectives must be adaptive and flexible. Your goals should change along with your channel. Always review your objectives in light of fresh information, emerging patterns, or shifts in the direction of your channel. For example, to maintain momentum, you could set a new, more ambitious objective if you've already exceeded your initial subscriber target ahead of time. On the other hand, if some objectives are becoming too difficult for you to achieve, change them to better suit your existing skills and resources.

While trying to establish your objective one thing you mustn't fail to do is maintaining motivation and recognizing accomplishments depending on the recognition and celebration of milestones. Celebrate your accomplishments, whether it's reaching your 1,000th subscriber milestone or seeing a notable rise in views. A sense of community and involvement can also be developed by sharing these accomplishments with your audience.

 Also, Every goal-setting cycle teaches important lessons that can guide future tactics. Consider the lessons you've learned from reaching and failing at your objectives. Make the most of this information to improve your strategy, execution, and general approach. For example, if a certain kind of content did very well, think about using similar components in other videos.

Lastly, Make sure that your objectives keep up with the expansion and development of your channel. Your goals should change to reflect new possibilities, difficulties, and audience preferences. Your efforts will continue to be relevant and effective if your aims are in line with the changing brand identity of your channel. You create the foundation for long-term growth and success on YouTube by establishing deliberate, strategic goals and putting an organized plan in place to achieve them. This meticulous procedure not only offers guidance but also cultivates an environment that values innovation and constant progress.

CHAPTER 3 : CONTENT CREATION

The first thing you need to gain proper knowledge of when it comes to content creation is video Production Basics,How do you go about Crafting Your Visual Masterpieces.NowVideo creation is a hybrid art and science that blends technological expertise and artistic vision. Every stage of the video production process, from ideation to filming and editing the finished result, is essential to producing interesting and captivating content. This comprehensive reference to the principles of video creation provides both useful guidance and creative inspiration.

First you need to work on Developing Your Vision Conceptually. Every excellent video begins with a well-defined idea. Start by generating concepts that connect with the theme of your channel and appeal to your intended viewership. Create an engaging narrative or message that will hold viewers' attention from beginning to end. Create a storyboard, which is a set of drawings or pictures that depicts each scene in your notion. This aids in mental organization, scene setup, and producing a coherent story. As an alternative, you can describe the precise angles and shots you want to get in a shot list. These are like a blueprint for your production, directing you and making sure nothing important is missed.

Secondly,Choose the Appropriate Equipments.The gear you choose has a big impact on how good your videos turn out. Below is a summary of necessary tools.Make an affordable and functional investment in a camera. Not just any camera but a really good one.While tiny cameras or smartphones with enhanced capabilities can potentially yield good results, DSLRs and mirrorless cameras offer the highest quality and flexibility in terms of image quality. When making your decision, take into account elements like resolution, frame rate, and lens compatibility.Also a video's audio can make or ruin it. Shotgun mics are perfect for concentrating on particular sounds, and lavalier mics are excellent for recording crisp conversations. If you want high-quality audio, think about getting an external microphone that reduces background noise and improves sound clarity. Creating visually appealing videos requires good lighting. Soft, diffused lighting improves the appearance and lessens harsh shadows. To evenly light your subject, use softboxes, ring lights, or natural light sources. Try out several lighting configurations to determine which ones will work best for your content. A steady shot is necessary to give an image a polished appearance. To avoid shaky footage and to keep your camera steady, use a tripod. To achieve smooth, fluid motion in dynamic shots or moving scenarios, think about utilizing a stabilizer or gimbal.

Thirdly you need to Get a Hang of Simple Filming Methods.Inorder to do that you need to follow These basic filmmaking strategies . Trust me it will totally improve the quality of your videos:

I).Composition: Use the rule of thirds to compose images that are harmonious and visually appealing. Using two horizontal and two vertical lines, divide your frame into a grid. Place important elements along these lines or at their intersections. This method draws the audience in and enhances the visual appeal.

II).Camera Angles: Play around with different angles to give your photos more depth and perspective. Low angles can make subjects appear strong or imposing, while high angles can convey a sense of fragility or supremacy. Changing perspectives aids in expressing various feelings and maintaining audience interest.

III).Depth of Field and Focus: Adjust the focus to blur the backdrop and accentuate your subject. Depth of field, or the range of distance that appears crisp in your shot, is affected by aperture adjustment. While a greater depth of field keeps more of the scene in focus, a narrow depth of field can highlight your subject.

IV).Movement: To give your footage more energy, use camera movement. You may increase the engagement of your movies by using techniques like tracking, tilting, and panning. For example, a tracking shot follows the action and draws the audience into the scene, while a slow pan might reveal details and increase suspense.

Fourthly you must consider Putting in Place Efficient Lighting.A strong tool for determining the tone and look of your video is lighting.
There are various lighting technique you can try out like:
I).Three-Point Lighting: Key light, fill light, and backlight are part of this traditional arrangement. The main source that illuminates the subject is the key light. The backlight creates depth by isolating the subject from the backdrop, while the fill light lessens the shadows cast by the key light. To get the desired effect, these lights can be positioned and their intensity changed.

II).Natural Lighting: A soft, natural effect can be achieved by using natural light. Place your subject close to windows or other sources of light, and use diffusers to lessen the intensity of the sun. Consider how the light will change during the day and schedule your shots appropriately.

Keeping uniform lighting requires an understanding of color temperature. Cool light gives an air of clarity and crispness, while warm light (measured in Kelvin) adds a warm, inviting feel. Make sure your lighting matches the tone and feel of your video, and if necessary, use gels or filters to change the color temperature.

Fifthly, A crisp, high-quality audio track improves the whole watching experience. To reduce background noise, record audio as close to the source as you can. To lessen plosive sounds, use pop filters, and keep an eye on the audio level to avoid distortion. Before you start recording, make sure everything is working as it should. Sound effects and music can increase the impact and mood of your video. Choose music that isn't restricted by copyright or write original tunes to go with your content. While editing, make sure background music doesn't drown out vital noises or dialogue by adjusting the volume.

Sixthly(FYI, I googled it and google said Sixthly is a word, so don't judge lol),you need to focus on Impact-Driven Editing.The process of editing gives your video its vitality. Utilise editing tools to combine video, improve images, and perfect audio.Cut out extraneous video to make your story more concise. Focus on pacing, ensuring that each scene flows smoothly and retains the audience's attention. Avoid extended, motionless shots unless they have a clear purpose. Use transitions to seamlessly connect distinct scenarios or shots. Choose transitions that fit the style of your video, whether it's a simple cut, a fade, or a wipe. Overusing flashy transitions can be distracting, so aim for subtlety and purpose. Adjust color balance, contrast, and saturation to give a professional effect. Color grading can generate a specific mood or ambiance, boosting the visual storytelling. Experiment with different color schemes to determine what best suits your content. Incorporate text overlays, lower thirds, and graphics to convey additional information or accentuate essential areas. Make sure the text is readable and consistent with the visual design of your brand. Utilise images selectively to prevent screen clutter.

Lastly, Make sure your film satisfies your standards by giving it a thorough inspection before publishing. Rewatch your video several times to identify any mistakes or discrepancies. Look for any inaccurate information, visual artifacts, or audio problems. Make the required modifications to guarantee a polished finish.
- Get input from others to learn about their viewpoints. Show your film to loved ones, coworkers, or friends, and take their feedback into account for any last adjustments. Make sure your movie is exported in the right resolution and format for the platform. For quick loading times and excellent visual fidelity, optimize file size and quality settings. To increase discoverability when posting to YouTube, provide pertinent titles, descriptions, and tags. Gaining an understanding of these fundamentals of video production can help you produce visually captivating and captivating material for your viewers. Every stage of the process, from planning and equipment selection to lighting, filming, and editing, adds to the final product's

impact and excellence. Delivering captivating stories and remarkable viewing experiences requires embracing innovation and accuracy in every facet of production.

Crafting Compelling Videos: The Art of Engaging Storytelling

To grab and hold viewers' attention, a compelling video must combine narrative elements, visual aesthetics, and emotional resonance in a way that goes beyond simple technical proficiency. This is a comprehensive look at how to make videos that grab attention and keep viewers watching all the way through.

A powerful story is the foundation of any visually appealing video. Start by outlining the main point or narrative you wish to share. Typically, a well-structured narrative consists of a Hook to Grab readers' attention right away with an engrossing opening. This might be a thought-provoking query, an unexpected detail, or an effective illustration. The intention is to stimulate interest and encourage viewers to continue watching. Then you need to apply Conflict or Problem. This is done by Describing the main issue or conflict that your film or content will try to resolve. This presents a problem that needs to be solved, which builds suspense and draws viewers in. At the end there must always be a resolution Resolution. You need to Provide a gratifying ending that settles the dispute or responds to the original query. Make sure the resolution adds value for the audience and is connected to the main point. Using these components to create a narrative arc keeps viewers interested and offers a compelling plot

 Having a well-written script is essential to effectively communicating your message. Begin with summarising the primary topics you wish to discuss, then develop these topics into in-depth conversation or storytelling. When penning your screenplay,Keep it Conversational.Write as though you're addressing your reader personally. Steer rid of jargon and speak simply and clearly. Your writing is easier to grasp and more relatable when it has a conversational tone.Inject Personality, Use your distinct voice and style to bring your story to life. This human touch makes your material stand out from the competition and strengthens the bond with viewers. Make a list of the images that will go with your conversation. This could include on-screen text, images, or descriptions of particular shots. A seamless and interesting viewing experience is ensured when your script is in line with visual clues.

A graphic planning tool called storyboarding helps you arrange each scene or shot in your video. Make a narrative to Visualise the Flow,To organize the flow of events, sketch or explain each scenario. This guarantees that all essential shots are included and aids in the visualization of the story's progression.Establish the flow of your scene changes. The rhythm and coherence of the video are preserved when transitions are planned ahead of time, whether they involve cuts, fades, or other effects. Coordinate with the Script,Make sure that the conversation and images flow naturally together by lining up your storyboard with the script. This collaboration makes your story come to life in a visually stunning video.

Your video's visual elements are crucial to drawing in and keeping viewers interested. Use a variety of strategies to improve your images. To provide variation and intrigue, try out various camera angles and perspectives. Use broad shots to provide context, or close-ups to highlight emotions. Use compositional guidelines, such as the rule of thirds, to produce well-balanced and eye-catching images. Make sure that the important components are positioned within the frame by paying attention to framing.

To add dynamism and direct the viewer's attention, use camera movement techniques including pans, tilts, and tracking views. Maintain the video's dynamic and engaging quality by timing your cuts to correspond with the cadence of your content.

Your video's opening and closing sequences are essential for leaving a lasting impression. Craft an engaging opening that establishes the tone for the rest of the piece. This could be an attention-grabbing sequence that captures the viewer's eye, a dramatic opening shot, or a succinct explanation of the video's goal.

Create a concluding section that reaffirms your point and implores viewers to take action. This could be a teaser for future material or a call to action (such as visiting your website or channel subscription). A summary or a branded outro are two examples of things that can make a lasting impression on viewers.

Your video's emotional impact and level of immersion are increased by the audio. Take into account the following components,Dialogue and Voiceover's. Make sure your dialogue and voiceovers are expressive and crystal clear. To express feelings and highlight important ideas, use your tone and intonation. Sound editing and appropriate mic placement can greatly enhance audio quality.Choose background music and sound effects that go well with the tone and subject matter of your video. While sound effects provide realism and intensity, music has the power to inspire emotions and improve the entire viewing experience

Adjust audio levels to guarantee a seamless blending of effects, music, and dialogue. Steer clear of loud music or distracting sound effects that overshadow the conversation. The impact and clarity of your audio are improved by proper mixing.

Your films will be more interesting if you include interactive and visual elements.Use animations, text overlays, and graphics to draw attention to key information or create visual appeal. Make sure these components don't overcrowd the screen and are in line with the aesthetic of your business. To promote viewer participation, make use of interactive elements like polls, clickable links, and annotations. These components have the power to increase audience engagement and offer them more value.

To produce a clean and interesting video, effective editing is essential.To keep your clips in a logical order, remove any extraneous content. Make sure the story flows naturally and that there are seamless transitions between scenes. To improve the visual aesthetic of your video, make adjustments to the color balance and grade it. A unified look and feel can be produced by using consistent color tones and visual effects.

For Final Touches,Check your film or content for any last-minute edits. Verify that all of the visual components are accurately aligned, that the audio levels are balanced, and that there are no continuity mistakes.Make sure your film satisfies your requirements by giving it a thorough evaluation before you finalize it: Rewatch your video several times to identify any mistakes or discrepancies. Look for any visual or audio problems, and fix them if needed.Show your video to others and ask them for their opinions. Giving yourself constructive criticism will help you gain important insights and complete your improvements. You may create films that capture viewers and communicate your idea by concentrating on these components. Every facet of video production, from crafting a fascinating story and writing captivating screenplays to utilising dynamic imagery and honing your final cut, goes into producing material that is both captivating and memorable. To improve your films and make a lasting impression on your audience, embrace innovation, meticulous attention to detail, and constant improvement.

CHAPTER 4: BUILDING YOUR AUDIENCE

To make sure your material reaches the people it is meant for, optimizing your videos for search is an essential tactic. You can augment the exposure of your video in search results, draw in new viewers, and expand your channel by doing so. This thorough tutorial covers both novel and cutting-edge methods for efficiently optimizing your videos, including utilizing metadata, comprehending YouTube's search algorithms, and interacting with viewers.

You need to Recognize the YouTube Search Algorithm. The order and placement of videos in search results are decided by YouTube's search algorithm. Videos that are most pertinent to the search query are given priority on YouTube. Numerous elements, including the video's title, description, tags, and content, are taken into consideration when determining its relevancy. Higher engagement metrics likes, comments, shares, and watch time tells YouTube that your video is worth watching. Higher-engagement videos have a better chance of ranking well in search results.

Users' watching histories and preferences are taken into account when YouTube tailors search results. This implies that different users may behave differently and that their prior interactions with related content may have an impact on how visible your video is.

Recently published material that discusses hot topics or emerging trends could rank higher in search results. Adding fresh videos and updating your material frequently will help you stay relevant in search results.

Also Formulating an Optimal Title is One of the most important components for search engine optimization is the title of the movie. An effective title should Incorporate Keywords,Use main keywords that correspond to the subject matter and setting of your film. To find terms that your target audience is likely to use, do some keyword research. Put words like "bake," "chocolate cake," and "recipe" in the title if your video or content is about "how to bake a chocolate cake. Be Clear and Descriptive,Craft a title that aptly sums up the information in the film. Steer clear of ambiguous or deceptive names, as they may result in increased bounce rates and decreased viewer satisfaction. Make use of attention grabbing and action-oriented language. Words like Essential, Ultimate,Guide, or Easy can improve your title's click-through rate and appeal.

Try to keep your title between 60 and 70 characters long. Long titles may be reduced in search results, which could lower click-through rates.

Craft a Captivating Summary Context and add extra information in the video description. This affects how your video gets indexed and ranked. Introduce yourself with a succinct synopsis that incorporates your main keywords. The purpose of this introduction should be to make it obvious why watching the video is worthwhile. Use headers, bullet points, or numbered lists to divide your explanation into sections. Users and search engines alike will find it simpler to scan and comprehend the information as a result.

 Throughout the description, include pertinent terms and secondary keywords. This facilitates the comprehension of the video's context and relevance to different search queries by YouTube's algorithm. Include timestamps and Links for important segments or subjects addressed in the video. Provide links to playlists, relevant information, or outside resources to improve user navigation and engagement.

In the description, provide a call-to-action (CTA) that invites readers to subscribe, like, remark, or share. Using CTAs to engage users can increase interaction and raise a page's search engine rating.

 By aiding in the classification and contextualization of your video, tags enable YouTube to more easily display your material in pertinent searches. Make sure your primary tags are closely related to the video's main subject. These ought to contain both your main keywords and their corresponding variations. Include subcategories or relevant topics in your secondary tags. This may increase the range of search terms in which your video comes up. For example, tags like "cake decorating," "baking tips," and "chocolate recipes" might be used in a content about making chocolate cake. You can also Include longer keyword phrases in your long-tail tags. Capturing particular search terms and specialized interests can assist you in reaching a wider audience. Examine the tags used in related or rival videos to obtain ideas and find more terms to add to your tags.

There's also a need to know How to Create a Catchy Thumbnail. Search engine click through rates are increased and viewers are drawn in by thumbnails. Produce aesthetically pleasing, high-resolution thumbnails that faithfully capture the essence of the content. To grab attention, use bold lettering, vivid colors, and striking pictures. To create brand identification and make your films instantly identifiable, develop a consistent style for your thumbnails. A unified visual presence is facilitated by the use of consistent colors, typefaces, and design components. Try out different thumbnail designs to determine which ones get the most click-throughs. A/B testing can reveal which visual components your audience responds to the best.

It's very important to make Use of Subtitles and Closed Captions as they both make content more searchable and accessible. You can either manually or automatically produce accurate captions on YouTube. Make sure the captions contain pertinent keywords and are in tune with the audio. To reach a wider, global audience, include subtitles in multiple languages. This can raise your video's search engine ranks and make it more visible in non-English speaking areas. - Since search engines may index captions and subtitles, incorporate relevant keywords and phrases into them. This can improve the relevancy of your video to different search terms.

Before uploading, rename your video files with catchy, keyword-rich names. A file called "chocolate-cake-recipe.mp4", for instance, has more information than "video1mp4". Always Verify that fields about playlists, video settings, and categories are filled out correctly. This makes your material more discoverable and aids YouTube in classifying it.

Keep an eye on critical performance metrics including watch duration, audience retention, sources of traffic, and click-through rates with YouTube Analytics. These metrics can be analyzed to gain insight into what is effective and what requires improvement. Adapt Strategies, Modify your video titles, descriptions, tags, and thumbnails by performance statistics to better suit search trends and audience preferences. Maintaining the effectiveness of your optimization efforts requires constant adjustments. Watch Trends, Keep up with modifications to search algorithms and developments in your industry. Over time, maintaining and enhancing your video's search presence can be achieved by adjusting to these adjustments.

Learn how to constantly Promote Interaction with the Audience Increasing audience interaction has a favorable effect on search rankings. Invite viewers to share the video and leave comments. Posts from communities and comments to viewers can increase visibility and interaction. Continually generate pertinent, high-quality content that appeals to your readers. Videos with high levels of engagement have a higher chance of being liked, shared, and commented on, all of which boost search rankings. Engage with your audience, hold live streams, and respond to comments to foster a feeling of community around your channel. The general engagement and search performance of your channel is improved by a devoted and vibrant community. Through the application of these sophisticated techniques for video search engine optimization, you can greatly increase the exposure and audience for your material. Optimizing your video's potential requires knowing YouTube's search algorithm, utilizing metadata, and interacting with viewers. All of these things are essential. Adopt these strategies to raise your video content's search engine results, draw in more viewers, and increase its success.

Marketing Your Channel

Clever Methods to Increase Visibility and Involvement Effective YouTube channel promotion requires a more complex strategy than just posting videos. It calls for a calculated fusion of offline and online strategies to increase exposure, draw in new viewers, and cultivate a devoted following. This extensive guide examines distinctive and detailed methods for channel promotion, guaranteeing a large and active viewership.

1). Creating a Unique Brand Identity:For marketing to be effective, a brand must have a strong and distinctive identity.Create a Differentiating Value Proposition.Clearly state what makes your channel special. Determine what makes you special, be it your personality, expertise, or area of interest in the material.

From graphic design to video content, every element of your channel should be consistent with your unique selling proposition (USP). Build Consistent Branding Elements,Create consistent visual components, like channel art, logos, and video thumbnails. Maintaining a consistent brand throughout your social media accounts and channels improves recognition and presents a businesslike image. Think about creating a style guide to ensure consistency in typefaces, color palettes, and graphic components. Create a Catchy Channel Name and Tagline.Select a catchy, easily spelled, and memorable channel name. Combine it with a succinct tagline that captures the spirit and value proposition of your channel. This strengthens the objective of your channel and makes it easy to recognize.

2). Making the Most of Social Media Platforms Social media is an effective tool for audience engagement and channel promotion. Cross-Promote on Multiple Platforms,Post links to your videos on Facebook, Instagram, LinkedIn, Twitter, and other sites. Make sure to customize your posts with relevant hashtags and formats to appeal to the users of each site. Use Twitter to interact with popular subjects and Instagram Stories for brief updates, for instance. Join and Participate in Relevant Communities.Interact with forums, communities, and groups that are associated with your area of expertise. When appropriate, share your material in these areas, participate in conversations, and offer value. Steer clear of spam and concentrate on developing sincere connections and providing insightful information. Run Social Media Campaigns,Create focused campaigns to increase channel visibility and traffic. Make use of platform-specific tools like Promoted Tweets on Twitter, Instagram Sponsored Posts, and Facebook Ads. To reach your ideal audience, target your adverts based on their interests, behaviors, and demographics.

3). Working Together with Other Creators: Working along with other YouTubers can bring new viewers to your channel.Find Possible Partners, Seek out content creators in your niche or who have complimentary styles. Look for creators whose followers fit your intended audience. Opportunities for collaboration may be joint videos, interviews, or special guest appearances on each other's channels.Pitch Creative Collaboration Ideas,Make suggestions for collaboration that will be advantageous to both sides. Think about forms such as co-hosted live streams, challenge videos, or group reviews. Make it obvious why the partnership is valuable and how it advances the objectives of both channels. Participate in Cross-Promotion,Share the content of your partners on your channel and vice versa. By exposing both channels to each other's audiences, this reciprocal promotion promotes mutual growth and enhanced visibility.

4).Making Use of Email Marketing Email marketing is a powerful tool for increasing traffic and cultivating a devoted audience.Create an Email List, Provide rewards for email subscribers, such as early access to films, free materials, or exclusive content. Utilise sign-up forms on your website and channel to obtain interested visitors' email addresses.Create Interesting Newsletters,Distribute newsletters regularly that include information on upcoming projects, new videos, and exclusive offers. To target the interests and preferences of a certain audience, personalize your emails and segment your list. Promote Exclusive Content,Send subscribers behind-the-scenes glimpses or exclusive content via email marketing. This improves the bond between you and your audience in addition to providing value.

5).Interacting with Your Viewers:Developing a close bond with your audience promotes word-of-mouth advertising and loyalty.Respond to Feedback and Comments.Participate in conversation with viewers by answering their remarks about your videos. Express gratitude for compliments and provide careful consideration to any queries or issues raised. Interacting with your audience creates a sense of community and shows them that you appreciate their opinions. Host Interactive Events,To engage with your audience directly, plan live streaming, Q&A sessions, or online get-togethers. These events provide you the chance to interact with viewers in real-time, connecting with them and answering any questions or concerns they may have.Promote User-Generated Content, Ask your viewers to produce and distribute channel-related content. Fan art, reaction videos, and video answers are a few examples of this. User-generated material improves community involvement while also promoting your channel.

6).Making Search Engine Optimisation:Search engine optimisation (SEO) can greatly increase how easily people can find your channel.Conduct Keyword Research,To find pertinent terms and phrases for your films, use resources like TubeBuddy or Google Keyword Planner. To improve searchability, naturally include these keywords in the titles, descriptions, and tags of your videos.Produce High-Quality, Search-Friendly material,Put your best effort into creating material that answers frequently asked queries, offers solutions, or delves into hot subjects. YouTube's algorithm is more likely to recommend and display relevant, high-quality material in search results.Make sure that the titles of your playlists, video tags, and channel descriptions are optimized with pertinent keywords. Playlists that are well-structured and have titles that are full of keywords increase search exposure and viewer engagement.

7). Making Use of Influencer Marketing: By using reputable voices in your niche, influencer marketing can help you reach a wider audience.Find Relevant Influencers,Do some research on influencers who are well-liked by members of your intended audience. Seek influencers whose material fits the theme and ideals of your channel. Create Relationships with Influencers,Send tailored pitches to influencers, emphasizing the mutual benefits of a partnership. To encourage their cooperation, think about providing cash, special access, or product samples. Monitor and Analyse Campaign Performance. Keep tabs on influencer partnerships' results to evaluate their effect on the expansion of your channel. To evaluate the success of your efforts, look at data like subscriber growth, traffic, and engagement.

8).Taking Part in Conferences and Industry Events: Exposure and networking opportunities are provided via industry events and conferences.Attend Relevant Events,Take part in trade exhibits, seminars, and workshops in your field that are relevant to your specialization. When it's appropriate, interact with other participants, pick the brains of experts, and present your channel. Network and Form Partnerships. Make connections with possible sponsors, partners, or collaborators during these events. Developing contacts with business leaders in the field can open up important doors for advancement and development. Share Event Content,Post on your channel and social media about the experiences you had at industry events. This shows your active participation in the sector and gives your readers more content.

9). Producing Interesting Content for Multiple Platforms Adding more material to different platforms can increase traffic and draw in new viewers.Repurpose material,Modify your video material for various platforms. For example, cut shorter segments for TikTok or Instagram Reels, or create blog entries based on the subjects of your videos. Repurposing content makes it easier to reach audiences with varying format preferences. Collaborate with Platforms, Form alliances with resources or platforms related to your area of expertise. For instance, if your channel is fitness-focused, work with companies who make exercise gear or applications to produce co-branded content. Use features unique to your platform, including Instagram Highlights, Community Posts, and YouTube Stories, to interact with viewers and advertise your videos.

10).Examining and Modifying Marketing Techniques:The secret to successful promotion is constant examination and adaptation.Examine the analytics and keep an eye on measures like the number of views, click-through rates, engagement rates, and growth in subscribers. Examine which marketing tactics work best and which ones require modification. Try out various advertising strategies, including changing up your email campaign techniques or social media posts.

To increase the efficacy of your promotional methods, make adjustments based on your analysis and testing. Adjust regularly to shifting audience inclinations, platform algorithms, and trends. An approach that is both strategic and complex is needed to promote your YouTube channel. You may increase your reach and build a vibrant community by concentrating on unique branding, utilizing social media, working with other producers, and interacting with your audience. Accept these distinct and all-encompassing approaches to improve the visibility of your channel, draw in new subscribers, and succeed in the long run in the cutthroat world of YouTube.

Creating a Connection and Loyalty with Your Audience

Maintaining an active, engaged channel and building a devoted community depend on your ability to interact with your viewers. Creating meaningful interactions with your audience that entice them to become active participants in your channel is a key component of effective audience engagement, which extends beyond simply replying to comments.

Building a community around your channel improves viewer loyalty and engagement.Find a voice that is genuine, dependable, and appealing to your viewers. Via your interactions and content, express your mission and values clearly. Having a distinct voice makes it easier to connect with viewers who have similar interests and morals. Invite viewers to offer thoughts, comments, and feedback to cultivate a culture of active engagement. Use surveys, polls, and Q&A sessions to get feedback on potential future material or interesting subjects. To demonstrate that you value the suggestions made by viewers, actively embrace them.Create a Welcoming Environment,Establish a welcoming, inclusive community in which viewers are at ease interacting. Establish unambiguous rules for polite behavior and limit conversations to keep the atmosphere welcoming and encouraging.

Make Use of Remarks and Input.Remarks offer insightful information and chances for direct interaction with viewers.Respond Thoughtfully and Timely,Interact with viewers by giving insightful, timely responses to their remarks. Answer queries, give credit when credit is due, and provide helpful criticism. Personalized answers foster further engagement by demonstrating to viewers how much their opinions are valued. Highlight Viewer Contributions,Incorporate viewer queries, comments, or reviews into your videos or postings on social media. Publicly recognizing viewers fosters community and encourages participation from others. Think about putting together a "Viewer Spotlight" section where you feature remarks that are thought-provoking or fascinating. Manage Negative Feedback Constructively. Respond to criticism with tact and compassion. Resolve issues or critiques amicably and steer clear of contentious debates. Take criticism as a chance to grow and demonstrate your appreciation for different viewpoints.

Organise Interactive Live Broadcasts.Deeper audience participation and real-time interaction are possible with live streaming.Arrange frequent live broadcasts covering subjects that your viewers will find interesting. Add interactive features like polls, live Q&A sessions, and real-time debates. Pre-publicize these events to ensure maximum attendance.Interact with Viewers During Streams, Actively engage viewers by answering their queries, acknowledging their presence, and replying to their comments. To encourage conversation and produce a lively, interesting experience, use live chat.Follow Up After Streams, Thank attendees and highlight important lessons learned following the live event. To sustain viewer interest and entice them to join in on future events, share highlights or standout moments from the stream.

You need to also Create a Multi-Platform Online Identity Interacting with your audience on several media improves visibility and connection.Cross-Promote Content, Post links to your YouTube videos on forums, blogs, and social media. Utilize pertinent hashtags and formats in your promotion campaign to cater to the audience on each platform. Invite your social media fans to subscribe to your YouTube channel and interact with your videos. Create Platform-Specific Content. Provide material that is customized to each platform's distinct characteristics. Use Twitter for real-time updates or Instagram Stories for behind-the-scenes looks. Creating compelling content for several platforms helps you maintain an engaged and interested audience. Engage your audience on the platforms where they are most engaged by using Share information that speaks to their interests, engage in dialogue and reply to comments. Having a presence across several platforms improves the relationship you have with viewers.

Create Interactive Media, it helps to improve the viewing experience and encourages viewer engagement.To promote viewer participation, use features like interactive cards, end screens, and clickable annotations. Make content that encourages viewers to take part in tasks, surveys, or tests associated with the subjects of your videos.Promote User-Generated Content, Ask visitors to produce and distribute channel-related content. Personal narratives, response videos, and fan art may fall under this category. Emphasizing content created by users helps to build a feeling of community and motivates more interaction.Plan giveaways or contests with explicit entry requirements about your material. By sharing your content, leaving comments on blogs, or submitting videos, you may get viewers to engage. Giveaways and contests create buzz and draw in new viewers.

Use Personalisation Techniques, Respond to viewers by name and make content that specifically addresses their issues or areas of interest. Make your interactions feel unique so that the audience feels noticed and valued. Produce material that is suited to particular viewer demographics or preferences. Make movies, for instance, that answer frequently asked questions or go into specialized subjects in response to viewer comments. Viewers respond more strongly to customized material, which promotes continuous engagement.Create Subscriber Relationships,Provide subscribers with unique discounts, early access to videos, and behind-the-scenes access in addition to exclusive content. Special perks let you build stronger relationships with your most devoted viewers.

Thé community features on YouTube provide you with more opportunities to interact with your audience.Make Use of Community Posts,Post updates, surveys, and behind-the-scenes videos on YouTube by using the

Community tab. Posts from the community let users communicate directly and notify readers about new videos or events.Involve with YouTube Stories,Use YouTube Stories to post succinct, interesting updates. Use this feature to show off your everyday activities or answer viewer questions to establish a more relaxed and natural connection with your audience. To promote binge-watching and continuous engagement, group your videos into playlists or series. Playlists provide a well-curated, seamless content journey that improves the viewing experience.

It is beneficial to track and evaluate engagement metrics to improve communication and strategy.Keep an eye on metrics like watch time, audience retention, likes, and comments with YouTube Analytics. Gain an understanding of viewer behavior and the success of your engagement campaigns by analyzing these metrics.

 To find out what content appeals to your audience the most, look for trends in engagement metrics. Recognize trends in the way viewers interact, then use this information to customize your engagement and content strategies. Let your analytics provide insights that inform ongoing adjustments to your engagement strategies. To improve viewer engagement and connection, try a variety of content formats, interactive techniques, and marketing strategies.

You may increase your reach and enhance your online efforts by implementing offline interaction methods. Take part in conferences, meetups, and industry events that are relevant to your niche. Networking with industry professionals and fans can boost your visibility and generate opportunities for meaningful connections. -

Organize live events or meetups where you can connect with your audience in person. These activities give you a unique opportunity to create relationships and strengthen your community. Partner with local businesses or groups for marketing or events. Collaborations can help you reach new audiences and create ties within your community.

Staying adaptive and innovative ensures continuous success in audience engagement.Regularly offer new content formats or interactive aspects to keep your audience engaged. Experiment with live streaming, virtual reality, or interactive videos to give novel experiences.

Continuously seek feedback from your audience to learn their preferences and interests. Use surveys, comment sections, and social media interactions to obtain feedback and improve your engagement methods.Keep up with industry trends and upcoming technology to stay ahead of the curve. Adapting to new trends and breakthroughs helps you keep relevance and continue engaging effectively with your audience.

Effective involvement with your audience is vital for developing a loyal and engaged community. By establishing a community culture, employing interactive content, and applying various engagement tactics, you may foster deeper connections and boost viewer loyalty. Adopt these all-inclusive strategies to build genuine relationships, stimulate participation, and guarantee your YouTube channel's long-term success.

CHAPTER 5: MONETIZING YOUR CHANNEL: DIVERSE STRATEGIES FOR REVENUE GENERATION

More than just turning on advertisements, YouTube channel monetization includes a range of tactics to generate long-term revenue sources. A combination of strategic planning, inventiveness, and utilizing several revenue streams to maximize profits are needed for effective monetization. This article offers a thorough road map for achieving financial success by exploring various and distinctive methods of channel monetization.

1). Ad Revenue: Making the Most of the AdSense Possibility For many YouTubers, ad money serves as their main source of income, however maximizing this revenue necessitates a sophisticated strategy. You need to first Comprehend AdSense Mechanics,I.e CPM (cost per thousand impressions), CPC (cost per click), and viewing demographics are some of the factors that determine AdSense revenue. Learn how these things affect your revenue and modify your content tactics accordingly. Produce top-notch, marketer-friendly video content that draws large audiences and stimulates increased CPM rates. Steer clear of contentious subjects that could restrict the placement of ads and concentrate on issues that suit the interests of advertisers.Increased ad income is frequently the result of higher engagement rates. To increase video ranks and draw in more sponsors, ask viewers to like, comment on, and share your content.

2).Brand alliances and sponsorships Beyond the typical ad revenue stream, sponsorships and brand collaborations offer significant opportunities. Look for businesses or brands associated with your specialty. Seek for partners whose goods and services fit the interests of your audience and your content. Examine their prior joint ventures and viewer interaction to determine suitability. Write comprehensive proposals that showcase the demographics of your channel's viewership, engagement statistics, and pertinent material. Present your value offer and explain how the collaboration will help both of you. Agree on terms that take into account the potential influence and power of your channel. Talk about deliverables like product reviews, sponsored content, and dedicated videos. Make sure the collaboration upholds the integrity and values of your brand.

3).Partner Promotion:By advertising goods or services, you can earn commissions through affiliate marketing.Pick affiliate networks that align with your target market and content. Seek programs that have a solid reputation, dependable tracking systems, and competitive commission rates.Give your material a natural, valuable feel by including affiliate links within it. Make tutorials, product evaluations, or advice that will help your audience. To determine which goods bring in the most money, track the effectiveness of affiliate links using tracking tools. To optimize profits, modify your advertising strategy in light of performance statistics.

4). Sales of Products and Merchandise*You might diversify your revenue streams by offering branded merchandise or digital products for sale. Create items that represent your channel's brand, including t-shirts, mugs, or hats. Reduce upfront costs by handling production and delivery with print-on-demand services. Provide digital goods such as downloadable books, access to online education, or unique content. Create goods that make use of your experience and give your target market more value.To advertise your digital goods and items, make use of your videos, social network accounts, and channel community features. To increase sales, emphasize the features and advantages that set your offerings apart.

5). Subscriptions and Memberships in Channels: Subscriptions and channel memberships offer benefits or access to unique content, which generates a consistent revenue stream.Make channel memberships available so that subscribers can receive special benefits. Emojis, badges, early access to content, and members-only films are a few examples of benefits. To appeal to various audience segments, establish membership tiers with differing amounts of benefits.Provide content that can be viewed only by subscribers by using services like YouTube's Super Thanks or Patreon. To increase engagement and loyalty, provide subscribers access to behind-the-scenes footage, special content, or interactive possibilities.Using your films, social media posts, and community posts, actively push membership alternatives. Emphasize the advantages of signing up to entice more viewers to become subscribers.

6). Donations and Crowdfunding:Donations and crowdsourcing allow you to get support from your audience and can be used to finance one-time events or continuous content production.Launch crowdfunding campaigns for certain initiatives, like a new video series or equipment upgrades, using websites like Kickstarter or Indiegogo. Clearly state your objectives and entice supporters with prizes. Create a contribution page on a website like PayPal or Ko-fi. In your community postings, channel banners, and video descriptions, include links to donate. Give donors rewards for their contributions, such as shoutouts or customized material. Express gratitude to contributors by mentioning their work in your content or on social media. Maintaining a solid rapport with funders promotes continued financial support.

7).Syndication and licensing:Opportunities to profit from content repurposing and redistribution are offered by licensing and syndicating: - Permit businesses, organizations, or other content producers to license your work for use in their initiatives. Sites like Storyful and Jukin Media can assist in overseeing license agreements and guaranteeing just recompense.Distribute your work to various media outlets or platforms. Republishing videos on affiliate websites, TV networks, or streaming services is one example of this. Make sure syndication agreements complement your income targets and content strategy.Make sure the terms you agree upon for licensing or syndicating content adequately represent the value of your work. Make sure agreements safeguard your intellectual property rights and provide fair pay.

8). Providing Advice or Services: Make money off of your knowledge by taking on freelance or consultancy work in your area of expertise. Identify Your area of Expertise and Make use of your abilities and knowledge to provide freelance or consulting jobs. This could involve advice relevant to a certain niche, social media management, content development, or video production. To advertise your consulting services, use social media and your channel. To prove your expertise and draw in new business, share case studies, success stories, and testimonials. Clearly state your service terms and pricing schedule. Give clients thorough information about what to expect from your services and how they might profit from them.

9). Organising Webinars and Workshops: You can earn money while sharing your skills by holding seminars and webinars. Arrange and conduct webinars or workshops covering subjects related to your speciality. Give participants insightful analysis, useful advice, or practical instruction. Establish admission costs for your webinars or workshops. Offer tiers of fees for varying access levels, such as basic attendance or premium packages with more features.Promote Your Event, Use email lists, social media, and your channel to advertise your webinars and seminars. Emphasize the advantages of coming and the value that attendees will receive.

10). Assessing and Modifying Monetisation Techniques:Constantly assessing and modifying monetization tactics guarantees steady revenue growth. Keep tabs on all revenue streams' performance to spot patterns and potential areas for development. Utilise analytics software to evaluate the merits of various monetization strategies. Try out novel monetization techniques and make necessary adjustments to tactics in light of your findings. To improve your strategy and increase profits, keep up with market developments and new prospects. Consult with your audience regarding potential revenue streams, such as products or memberships. Utilize their suggestions to improve services and customer happiness.

Your YouTube channel needs to be monetized strategically and in a variety of ways. You may create a sustainable business model by utilizing sponsorships, affiliate marketing, goods, ad revenue, and other revenue streams. Maintaining long-term success and growth requires regular strategy evaluation and adaptation. Adopt these all-inclusive strategies to accomplish your monetization objectives and build a solid financial base.

Maintaining Motivation and Preventing Burnout:

Methods for Continuing Well-Being and Creativity Establishing and sustaining a prosperous YouTube channel may be an immensely challenging yet thrilling experience. Long-term success requires striking a balance among creativity, productivity, and personal well-being.

Establishing a routine that is both flexible and organized is essential to sustaining motivation and avoiding burnout. Create a Realistic Timetable,Plan out your content production in a way that complements your personal and professional objectives. Allow time for rest, filming, editing, and ideation. Make sure your timetable is reasonable to prevent overcommitting yourself. Sort your tasks into smaller, more doable categories. Prioritise high-impact chores and deal with less important ones when things aren't as busy. This lessens stress and aids in workload management.

Implement Time Management Techniques.Make use of time-blocking and the Pomodoro Technique, among other time-management strategies. These techniques can improve productivity and focus, enabling you to go at a steady pace without getting overwhelmed.

Set long-term targets like reaching a milestone or branching out into new content areas, as well as short-term ones like hitting a monthly target of views or subscriptions. This well-rounded strategy helps you stay motivated and focused. Keep a close eye on your advancement towards these objectives and mark any accomplishments, no matter how tiny. Acknowledging your successes gives you a sense of satisfaction and inspires you to keep going. Be ready to modify your objectives in light of your changing circumstances and demands. Setting goals with flexibility helps you stay realistic and prevents you from setting yourself up for failure

Always Put Self Care and Well-Being Into Practice. Making self-care a priority is crucial for long-term success and avoiding burnout:Make time in your schedule for rest. Take part in enjoyable things outside of content creation, such as hobbies, physical activity, or quality time with loved ones. This supports your creative and energetic renewal.Take care of your physical well-being by eating a balanced diet, working out frequently, and getting enough rest. A fit body promotes mental clarity and improves general well-being. Clearly define the lines separating your personal and professional lives. Steer clear of working too long hours or checking work-related chores after specified hours. Establishing limits aids in keeping work from invading your time.

Create a network of encouraging people can boost motivation and reduce stress. Establish connections with other content producers to collaborate and offer support to one another. Feelings of loneliness can be lessened and insightful insights can be gained by sharing experiences, counsel, and support.

Consult mentors or advisors who can provide helpful criticism and direction. Their viewpoint and experience can guide you through obstacles and maintain motivation.

Engage with your viewers and reply to their comments to help create a community around your channel. Developing a rapport with your audience fosters a positive atmosphere and offers inspiration through their comments and involvement.

Adaptability and receptivity to change is beneficial for handling obstacles and sustaining motivation. Be ready to modify your plans and strategies in response to changing trends, user input, or individual situations. Accepting flexibility makes it easier to handle unforeseen difficulties and maintain the relevance of your material. To keep your channel interesting and lively, experiment with different content formats, styles, or subjects. You may avoid boredom and rekindle your enthusiasm for content development by experimenting.

See setbacks as chances for improvement as opposed to failures. Examine what went wrong, draw lessons from the experience, and apply the knowledge gained to make better attempts in the future.

To avoid burnout and preserve creativity, effective stress management is essential. Make stress-reduction activities a part of your daily routine. Some examples include mindfulness, meditation, and deep breathing exercises. These techniques can support mental clarity and anxiety management.

Take into account assigning or outsourcing labor-intensive projects or ones that fall outside of your area of expertise. You can lessen your workload and concentrate on creative activities by hiring independent contractors to do administrative, graphic design, and editing duties.

Aim for greatness, but stay away from the perfectionism pit. Realize that not all of your content has to be perfect. Stress and anxiety can be released by accepting flaws.

Sustaining motivation requires preserving originality and inspiration.Continually Seek Inspiration.Interact with a variety of media, such as podcasts, films, books, and other content producers. Being exposed to a variety of inspiration sources might help you stay creative and generate fresh concepts. Try out creative activities like vision boards, brainstorming sessions, and group projects. Taking part in these activities might inspire creativity and offer new insights. Continually remind yourself of the reasons behind your channel's launch and the things that make you passionate about creating content. Motivating yourself again can come from rekindling your passion.

Realistic expectations can also help avoid fatigue and feelings of inadequacy. Acknowledge that creating a profitable channel requires time and work. Be reasonable with your expectations for revenue, audience engagement, and growth rates. Refrain from comparing yourself to other people and concentrate on your journey.

Inform your audience of any modifications to your content plan clearly and concisely. It is easier to control audience expectations and less stressful for you when you communicate clearly.

Note and honor minor victories attained along the route. Acknowledging small victories inspires people and rewards good behavior.

Seeking professional assistance when necessary can help manage mental health and avoid burnout. You should think about seeing a mental health professional if you're feeling particularly stressed, anxious, or burned out. Counseling or therapy can offer methods and encouragement for maintaining mental health.

Take advantage of resources like self-help books, online courses, or support groups that are devoted to well-being and stress management. These sites can provide further coping mechanisms and methods.

Creating long-term vision aids in keeping you motivated and coordinating your efforts with your key objectives.Define Your Vision and Purpose,Clearly state your channel's long-term goals and objectives. A clear vision gives you direction and inspiration, which keeps your attention on your objectives.

Set benchmarks and assess your progress towards your long-term goal regularly. You can keep in line with your objectives and make any adjustments by routinely evaluating your progress. As your channel develops and changes, be willing to adjust your objectives and vision. Accept fresh chances and be prepared to modify your approaches to remain inspired and current.

Sustaining your passion and preventing fatigue are essential for your YouTube channel's long-term success. You may adopt a balanced approach to content creation by prioritizing self-care, setting realistic goals, creating a sustainable routine, and asking for help when needed. To maintain ongoing creativity and well-being, embrace flexibility, learn how to efficiently manage stress, and maintain your inspiration. You may maintain your enthusiasm for content development and attain long-term success by putting these techniques into practice.

CHAPTER 6: LEGAL AND ETHICAL CONSIDERATION

To stay out of trouble with the law and protect intellectual property rights, YouTube content creators must understand the ins and outs of copyright and fair use. Knowing these ideas guarantees that you are not violating the rights of others while also assisting in the protection of your creative output. This comprehensive reference on copyright and fair use is intended for content creators who want to remain knowledgeable and compliant.in other to do this we must First understand what copyright is all about

What is copyright ?

Copyright is a legal privilege that gives the author of original works exclusive control over how their works are reproduced, distributed, and shown. A vast variety of creative works, including films, music, books, artwork, and more, are covered under this right.

Rather than the ideas themselves, copyright protection extends to a particular expression of those ideas. For example, the idea of a food show is not protected, but a video screenplay is. Each jurisdiction has a different term for copyright protection.

For instance, copyright in the United States normally lasts for the author's lifetime plus an additional 70 years. The term applies to anonymous or works created for hire, and it is 95 years from the date of creation or 120 years from the date of publication, whichever is sooner. Owners of copyright own the sole authority to duplicate, disseminate, exhibit, perform, and develop derivative works that draw inspiration from the original work. These rights can be sold or licensed, and they are transferable.

Next up. We need to understand the concept of Fair Use. Fair Use is a legal theory that, under some circumstances, permits restricted use of copyrighted content without the owner's consent. It is intended to strike a balance between the public interest in freedom of expression and the rights of producers.

Five criteria are used to assess fair usage in the United States:

I).Purpose and Character: Whether the use is for profit-making or charitable educational objectives. It is more likely that transformative applications that introduce fresh expression or meaning will be regarded as fair use.

II).Character of the Copyrighted Work: The type of work that is being utilized. Compared to creative works, the use of factual or non-fiction content is more likely to be considered fair use.

III).Amount and Substantiality: The percentage of the source material that is utilized. It is more likely to be considered fair use to use a minor, non-essential portion of the work.

IV).Impact on the Market:How the original work's market is affected by its utilization. It is less likely to be considered fair use if the usage diminishes the original work's market value or eliminates the need for it.

V).International Context: The principle of fair use originated in the United States. Other nations have their laws governing copyright infringement, such as the UK, Canada, and Australia's "fair dealing" provisions. It's critical to comprehend the particular copyright regulations that apply in your area.

Producers Often, content creators interact with copyrighted material in ways that could be considered fair use. Fair use might include, for instance, using Content snippets to examine a review's themes. Producing fresh works that satirically or humorously parody the source material. If parodies blatantly alter the source material into something new, they frequently qualify as fair use.

Also using copyrighted content in tutorials or lectures falls under the category of fair use in some situations, particularly when the content is being utilized for research or instruction.

Fair use can also be used for News Reporting. Adding context or examples to news reporting by utilizing copyrighted content. Fair use is frequently employed in the context of news reporting, especially when the content is used to inform the public.

Preventing Violations of Copyright
Take into account the following procedures to safeguard oneself against accusations of copyright infringement:

I). Use Copyright-Free work: Whenever possible, choose work that is in the public domain or is free of royalties. Numerous platforms provide content that can be used without worrying about violations of copyright.

II).Get Permissions: Consult the copyright holder for permission before utilizing any content that is protected by copyright. This may entail negotiating license agreements or securing formal approval for particular applications.

III).Produce Original stuff: Don't rely on stuff that is protected by copyright; instead, create original content. Creating original content and ideas aids in defining your brand's identity and preventing copyright issues.

IV).Attribute Properly: Make sure you provide due credit to the original creators of any content you use if it calls for it. Adhere to the license's attribution specifications.

YouTube has its standards and resources for handling copyright concerns. Videos with copyrighted content are automatically identified and managed by YouTube's Content ID system. Your video may be removed from the platform or subject to limitations on its ability to be monetized if the system receives a claim that it includes copyrighted content. If your channel consistently violates copyright policies, you may be subject to copyright strikes. Channel termination may occur if three strikes are accumulated in ninety days. It is imperative to comprehend and abide by copyright regulations to prevent strikes.

You can use YouTube's platform to contest a Content ID assertion if you think it is inaccurate. Provide context and supporting data to back up your assertion, and be ready to go to court if the disagreement gets out of hand.

Copyright law can be complicated, thus it's usually a good idea to consult an expert. You should think about speaking with intellectual property attorneys or other legal specialists for comprehensive advice on copyright and fair use. They can guide you through certain legal challenges and offer tailored guidance. To enhance your comprehension of copyright laws and fair use principles, make use of educational resources like webinars, online courses, and legal manuals.

Copyright rules and laws are subject to change. To guarantee continuous compliance, stay up to date on modifications to copyright laws and recommended procedures. For content creators , upholding ethical standards is crucial even beyond legal compliance

When using someone else's creation, always think about the moral ramifications. Give credit where credit is due and acquire the required permits to honor the rights and labors of other authors. Promote a responsible and respectful culture in your community. To encourage understanding and adherence to legal norms, educate your audience and other creatives on copyright and fair use. Make an effort to produce original work and offer fresh viewpoints and ideas to the creative community. Being original not only helps you stay out of trouble with the law, but it also builds your reputation and brand. YouTube content makers must grasp and navigate fair use and copyright to conduct business legally and morally. Understanding these ideas thoroughly, upholding intellectual property rights, and putting best practices into action can help you safeguard your creations, stay out of trouble with the law, and support the creative community.

Handling Privacy and Security

Crucial Techniques for YouTubers YouTube video creators must strike a balance between the need to interact with their audience and protecting their safety and privacy. Because the site is public, you run the danger of privacy violations and security issues, among other things.

This comprehensive guide will help you manage privacy and safety so that you can have a safe and secure online presence:

1).Recognizing Privacy Risks Security flaws and the possible exposure of personal information are the privacy risks for YouTube creators. Effective protection starts with an awareness of these threats. You may unintentionally put yourself in danger by disclosing information about your whereabouts, everyday activities, or personal affairs. It is possible to track your whereabouts or have unauthorized access to your personal information using this information.

There is also a chance that someone will try to access your devices and accounts. Cybercriminals might target your channel or related accounts in an attempt to compromise your business or steal confidential data. Being visible online might draw negative attention, such as harassment and stalking. Large-follower creators are particularly susceptible to these kinds of dangers

2). Protecting Your Accounts Online
 Safeguarding your internet accounts is essential to avoid unwanted access and any security lapses. Use Strong Passwords, Make sure your account passwords are complicated, combining special characters, numbers, and letters. Don't use facts that can be guessed at, like birthdays or well-known phrases.Activate Two-Factor Authentication (2FA)To increase security, enable 2FA on each and every one of your accounts. This usually entails

getting your password and a verification code on your mobile device.

Keep a close eye on your account activity logs to look for any unusual activity. Deal with any strange activity or unauthorized logins right away. Update your operating system and applications, and install antivirus software. This aids in defending your gadgets against security risks and infections.

3. Handling Private Data:Restricting the quantity and kind of personal data you disclose online is essential to protecting your privacy.Limit Personal Details. Refrain from sharing particulars about yourself in your films or social media posts, such as your home location, phone number, or a rundown of your everyday activities.Make sure you routinely check and modify the privacy settings on your social media platforms and YouTube channel. Limit who can connect with you and read your material. Make sure third-party services or programs you use are trustworthy and do not ask for undue access to your data. Use a Business Email,Establish a different email account specifically for correspondence about business and

content. This contributes to the security and privacy of your private email.

4).Safeguarding Your Intellectual Property and Content: To stop illegal use and infringement, you must secure your intellectual property and material.Watermark Your Videos,To prevent unauthorized usage and guarantee that your content is always identified as yours, add watermarks to your videos.Understand Copyright policy, Make sure your material conforms with these rules by familiarising yourself with YouTube's copyright policy. You can get even more protection by registering your original work with copyright authorities.Look up your content online regularly to spot any unauthorized use. Tracking the usage of your content can be facilitated by using tools such as Google Alerts.

5. Handling Cyberbullying and Mistreatment: Taking action against cyberbullying and harassment is essential to preserving a secure and encouraging atmosphere. Make sure to Report Abuse,To report any harassment or abusive behavior, use the reporting options on YouTube.

This includes offensive remarks, menacing correspondence, or damaging information directed at you or other people.Restrict or block people who behave abusively using the moderating tools. Additionally, you can configure filters to automatically remove offensive comments from your channel. Seek Support If you get extreme harassment or threats, get in touch with friends, family, or professional counselors. Support is crucial for coping with the emotionally draining nature of cyberbullying.

6). Protecting Your Security:It is important to take precautions for your online and offline safety to ensure your safety. Avoid Sharing Location Information,Don't share your exact location or post updates about your whereabouts in real-time. This reduces the possibility of being followed or found by someone who has bad intentions.Be Wary of Meetups, If you're planning to meet fans or collaborators in person, pick areas that are open to the public and think about bringing a friend along. Prioritise safety above everything else, and share personal information with caution. Educate Yourself on

Safety Measures, Keep up to date on recommended practices and potential risks related to internet safety. Being aware of phishing efforts, popular frauds, and security precautions might help you avoid potential problems.

7). Taking Care of Your Online Image: Sustaining a favorable virtual image is crucial for both individual and occupational development. Be Aware of Public Perception, Think about how the public and your audience could interpret your words and deeds. In both your interactions and material, strive for professionalism and deference. Address Negative Feedback Constructively, React positively or constructively to criticism or unfavorable comments. Steer clear of contentious debates and concentrate on handling situations professionally and with respect. Maintain Consistency, Make sure that your brand identity and personal values are reflected throughout your online presence. Maintaining consistency in both your messaging and behavior fosters credibility and trust among your target audience.

8). Formulating a Plan for Crisis Management Being ready for future emergencies guarantees that you can manage them skillfully.Create a Response strategy. Draft a crisis management strategy that outlines what to do in case of harassment, security breach, or other emergency. Provide the legal or security professionals contact details.Interact with Your Audience,Be open and honest with your audience if a crisis affects your channel or public perception. While addressing issues, give updates that are honest and transparent. Evaluate and Improve,Examine your response to a crisis and note any areas that need improvement. Apply the things you've learned to improve your safety and privacy safeguards.

9).Making Use of Professional and Legal Resources: Having access to professional and legal resources can offer further security and direction.Get guidance from attorneys who focus on internet safety, intellectual property, and privacy. They can offer customized advice and support as you work through challenging situations. Become a member of associations for digital media and content creation . These groups frequently provide tools, instruction, and assistance in resolving privacy and security issues. Remain Up to Date on Legal Developments, Stay informed about modifications to privacy laws and regulations. Being aware of new legal requirements aids in maintaining your compliance and safety.

10).Encouraging a Respectful and Safe Online Community:A pleasant environment is created in your community by promoting a culture of safety and respect.Set Clear Guidelines,Clearly define and disseminate community standards for conduct and relationships. Encourage an environment that is inclusive, polite, and makes everyone feel comfortable. Set a Good Example, Act with decency and morality in your communications and material. Your behavior shapes the culture of your community and sets the tone for it. Invite others to report offensive language or content. Give precise instructions on how to file reports of problems, and make sure that these are handled seriously.

As a YouTube creator, managing privacy and security requires forethought, knowledge, and proactive actions. You can establish a safer and more regulated online presence by being aware of privacy risks, protecting your accounts, handling personal information, and dealing with online harassment. By putting these procedures into place, you can safeguard your overall well-being, intellectual property, and personal safety while concentrating on producing interesting material in a polite and safe atmosphere.

Ethical Content Creation

Responsible Media Principles and Practices In a time when digital content permeates every aspect of our lives, producing ethical content is essential to responsible media and goes beyond simple legal compliance. Adhering to ethical standards builds credibility, builds audience trust, and benefits the online community of

YouTube creators. This is a thorough guide to producing ethical material, with an emphasis on values and procedures that preserve honesty and decency.

In content creation, authenticityrefers to expressing yourself and your message honestly, without embellishment or deceit. Make any sponsorships, alliances, and paid promotions explicitly known. When the material is sponsored or you have a financial interest in promoting an item or service, your audience should know. By being open and honest, this transparency protects viewers from deceit. Steer clear of making false claims about goods, services, or firsthand encounters. Give correct data and make sure any assertions you make can be independently verified. Being truthful in reviews and opinions supports your reputation and shows consideration for the intellect of your audience.Preserve your moral character both personally and professionally by abstaining from sensationalism and clickbait. Make sure the title, thumbnail, and descriptions of your content appropriately convey the substance of the video.

To create ethical content, one must respect intellectual property rights, which entails recognizing and correctly utilizing the labor of others. When using any content including pictures, songs, or videos give due credit to the original authors. When appropriate, provide a link back to the source and follow the creator's or license's required attribution standards. Make sure that no copyrighted material is violated by your content. When employing copyrighted material, use materials that are licensed or royalty-free and get the required consent. Learn about copyright rules so that you can properly negotiate these boundaries. Make an effort to produce original material instead of mostly depending on the thoughts or writings of others. Being unique promotes creativity and shows regard for the creative process.

Upholding moral principles and safeguarding people's data depend on respecting privacy. Before disclosing a person's identity or photographing them, get their express consent. Make sure to heed demands for privacy and refrain from disclosing private information without authorization. Treat delicate subjects with consideration and decency. Consider the effects that your content may have on those who are interested in or impacted by the topic. When releasing content on sensitive topics, think about the possible outcomes. Preserve your audience's and your collaborators' personal information. Respect data privacy laws and refrain from disclosing or processing personal data improperly.

Make sure to always create content that honors the diversity of viewpoints and represents inclusivity improves the digital media environment. Make an effort to include a range of perspectives in your writing. To represent a wide range of identities and opinions, highlight a variety of voices, thoughts, and experiences. Take care to avoid reinforcing prejudices or preconceptions in your content by using language and imagery carefully. Make sure that no group of individuals is marginalized or misrepresented in your work. Add features like audio descriptions, subtitles, and accessible web design to make your material accessible to a larger audience. Ensuring that your content is accessible to all viewers, including those with impairments, is a priority.

Creating ethical content requires being aware of and in control of the wider social consequences of your work. Provide content that encourages productive discourse and makes a beneficial contribution to societal challenges. Handle subjects sensibly and refrain from disseminating inaccurate or dangerous information.Provide information in a thoughtful and balanced way to encourage critical thinking. Instead of taking something at face value, encourage your audience to investigate, ask questions, and find out more. Make advantage of your platform to back social projects and charitable causes. Changing the world for the better and bringing significant issues to people's attention can increase your influence and improve society.

To monetize your material ethically, your revenue-generating process must be open and equitable. Identify and disclose any product placements, sponsored content, and affiliate links. Make sure that any financial incentives associated with the content your audience views are communicated to them. Steer clear of using delicate or sentimental subjects for financial advantage. Make sure that your content's ethical standards are not jeopardized by your monetization techniques. Make sure that other creators or contributors are fairly compensated for their labor and services when working together. To create a fair and happy workplace, keep your word and fulfill your obligations.

A crucial component of producing ethical content is taking responsibility for your work and appropriately owning up to errors. Immediately own your mistakes and correct any inaccurate material you may have published. Being open and honest about mistakes fosters trust and shows a dedication to truthfulness and morality. React positively to comments and critiques. Consider it a chance for development and progress, and respond to criticism with civility and an open mind. Make sure your content creation procedures are up to date with ethical standards by regularly reviewing and improving them.

Keep up with industry advancements and best practices to guarantee continued adherence to moral standards.

Your content's ethical component is enhanced when you interact with and educate your audience. Provide your audience with instructional or interesting stuff that enhances their lives. Make sure the information or skills your content imparts are beneficial and go beyond mere amusement. Promote courteous and open communication in your neighborhood. Establish discussion areas where viewers can express their opinions, pose inquiries, and have deep dialogues.Encourage media literacy among your audience by teaching them how to critically think, verify facts, and identify reliable sources. Encouraging viewers to become knowledgeable media consumers promotes moral behavior.

Consider the ethical ramifications of your content creation and publication before you post it to guarantee ethical behavior.Before your content goes online, conduct an ethical review. Examine the material's possible effects, ethical issues, and wider ramifications. Ask counselors, mentors, or peers for their opinions on the moral implications of your writing. Outside viewpoints can offer insightful information and assist in spotting any problems. Consider your basic beliefs and how your content development methods relate to them regularly. Make sure that your job always demonstrates your dedication to moral principles. Creating ethical content requires a dedication to social responsibility, sincerity, and respect. By following these guidelines, you may improve the digital media environment while also fostering credibility and confidence. Maintaining integrity in all facets of your work necessitates constant introspection, openness, and contemplation as you navigate the intricacies of creating ethical content.

Appendices

Creating high-quality YouTube content requires a range of tools, software, and services. Below is a curated list of resources to help you in various aspects of content creation and management:

1).Content Creation Tools

A).Cameras:
  Sony ZV-1: A compact camera designed for vlogging with excellent autofocus and image quality.
  Canon EOS R: A mirrorless camera offering high-resolution video and advanced features for professional-quality content.

B).Microphones:
  Rode VideoMic Pro: A shotgun microphone ideal for capturing clear audio in video production.

Blue Yeti: A versatile USB microphone known for its high-quality sound, suitable for voiceovers and podcasts.

C).Lighting:
 Elgato Key Light: Adjustable LED lighting that provides consistent, high-quality illumination.

 Neewer Ring Light Kit: An affordable ring light for even and flattering lighting in your videos.

2). Video Editing Software

A).Adobe Premiere Pro: Industry-standard video editing software with extensive features for professional editing.

B).Final Cut Pro X: A powerful video editing tool for Mac users, offering advanced editing and color correction capabilities.

C).DaVinci Resolve: A comprehensive editing suite with a free version that includes professional-grade color correction and editing tools.

3).Graphic Design and Thumbnails

A).Canva: A user-friendly design tool for creating custom thumbnails, channel art, and other graphics.

B).Adobe Photoshop: Advanced software for detailed graphic design and image manipulation.

4).SEO and Analytics

A).TubeBuddy: A browser extension that provides tools for optimizing your YouTube channel, including keyword research and analytics.

B).VidIQ: A platform offering video SEO tools, competitor analysis, and real-time performance insights.

5).Social Media Management

A).Hootsuite: A comprehensive tool for scheduling and managing social media posts across multiple platforms.

B).Buffer: An easy-to-use social media management tool for planning and tracking your social media content.

6). Collaboration and Project Management

A).Trello: A project management tool that helps you organize tasks, track progress, and collaborate with team members.

B).Asana: A platform for managing projects, assigning tasks, and monitoring workflows.

Glossary of Terms

Understanding key terms is essential for mastering YouTube and digital marketing. Here's a glossary of commonly used terms:

YouTube Terms**

- **AdSense**: Google's advertising program that allows creators to earn money from ads displayed on their videos.
- **Content ID**: YouTube's system for detecting and managing copyrighted material in videos.
- **CPM (Cost Per Thousand Impressions)**: A metric that represents the cost an advertiser pays for every 1,000 impressions of an ad.
- **CTR (Click-Through Rate)**: The percentage of viewers who click on a video after seeing its thumbnail and title.

- **End Screen**: A feature that allows creators to add interactive elements at the end of their videos, such as links to other videos or subscription buttons.
- **Monetization**: The process of earning revenue from your content through ads, sponsorships, or other means.

2.2 Digital Marketing Terms

- **SEO (Search Engine Optimization)**: The practice of optimizing content to rank higher in search engine results and attract more organic traffic.
- **Engagement Rate**: A metric that measures the level of interaction (likes, comments, shares) relative to the number of followers or views.
- **ROI (Return on Investment)**: A performance measure used to evaluate the efficiency of an investment, calculated by comparing the profit to the cost of the investment.
- **Affiliate Marketing**: A marketing arrangement where you earn a commission for promoting other companies' products or services.

- **A/B Testing**: A method of comparing two versions of a piece of content to determine which performs better in terms of user engagement or conversion rates.

3. Sample Content Calendar

A content calendar is a valuable tool for planning and organizing your video content. Here's a template to help you manage your content schedule:

Date	Video Title	Description	Status	Platform	Notes
01/01/2024	How to Start a YouTube Channel	A beginner's guide to launching a channel.	Planned	YouTube	Include tips for equipment
01/08/2024	Editing Tips for Beginners	Basic editing techniques for new creators.	In Production	YouTube	Use screen recordings

01/15/2024	The Best Microphones for Vlogging	Review of top vlogging microphones.	Scheduled	YouTube	Contact brands for samples
01/22/2024	YouTube SEO Strategies	How to optimize videos for search engines.	Planned	YouTube	Research recent algorithm updates
01/29/2024	Monthly Q&A Session	Answering viewer questions and feedback.	Not Started	YouTube	Collect questions from social media

Instructions for Use:

- **Date**: Schedule the date for publishing or filming the video.
- **Video Title**: Draft a working title for the video to keep your content focused.
- **Description**: Write a summary of the video's content and key points.
- **Status**: Track the progress of each video (e.g., Planned, In Production, Scheduled, Completed).

- **Platform**: Specify where the video will be published (e.g., YouTube).
- **Notes**: Add any additional information or tasks related to the video, such as collaborating with others or sourcing materials.

Using this content calendar template helps ensure consistent content production, organization, and strategic planning, making it easier to manage your channel and stay on track with your content goals.

Conclusion

It's evident by the end of "YouTube Secrets Revealed: Master the Algorithm, Boost Your Views, and Monetize Like a Pro"
that achieving success on the platform is just as difficult as it is rewarding. We have journeyed through the complexities of video development, audience engagement, and strategic growth, providing you with a road map to realize your YouTube dreams. There isn't a one-size-fits-all recipe or strategy for success on YouTube. Rather, it is a synthesis of imagination, planning, and tenacity. A strong foundation for your journey is provided by the information you've received from comprehending the ecosystem of the platform, organizing and planning your content, improving the quality of your videos, and developing and interacting with your audience.

Think back on the ethical content creation guidelines and the legal issues we covered. These not only protect your channel but also help you establish long-lasting credibility with your peers and viewers. Accept these ideas as essential to your strategy and make sure that honesty and decency serve as the cornerstones of your success.

Recall that YouTube growth is an ever-changing process. Audience tastes fluctuate, trends change, and algorithms adapt. You can stay ahead of the curve by continuing to learn new things and being flexible. To improve your strategy, review and adjust your strategies regularly, try out new content ideas, and constantly ask for feedback. In the end, the most prosperous YouTubers are those who never waver from their commitment to their objectives, resilience in the face of difficulty, and love for what they do.

 Your greatest strengths are your distinct voice and vision. Utilize them to produce content that stands out in the cluttered digital scene and has a profound emotional connection with your audience. keep inspired, keep focused, and never undervalue the power of your hard work and originality as you start your YouTube journey.

There are a tonne of opportunities waiting to be discovered in the huge and vibrant digital world. By using the knowledge and resources found in this guide, you will be well-equipped to successfully negotiate this fascinating territory and leave your mark. I appreciate you coming along to learn about the science and art of being a popular YouTuber. Your journey has just begun; seize it with zeal and commitment, and let your desire propel you forward to new heights. The days of becoming a YouTube creator are coming.

www.ingramcontent.com/pod-product-compliance
Lightning Source LLC
Chambersburg PA
CBHW050259230526
45471CB00005B/1948